Expect Good Things

Written and
Illustrated by
Lynne Gerard

The C.R. Gibson Co. · Norwalk · CT · 06856

Feelings
of loneliness
pass,
just as
winter gives
way to
spring.

You will find
your way
to happiness
like a seedling
finds its way
to the sun,
by growing
and changing
and pressing
on.

The day
you were born,
somewhere a flower
bloomed, the sun shone
even brighter, and
when the wind
moved over the
ocean, it whispered
your name...

You are a
special person,
and the world
is a better place
because
you
are
in it.

Whenever you
smell the rain,
or hear a
birdsong, or
see a butterfly
in the sun, you
will know someone
is thinking of
you and wishing
you a peaceful
feeling.

When storm clouds
darken your world,
remember friendship offers
a safe harbor where you
are never alone... there you
will find comfort and
support and understanding.

Days that
are cold
and grey
and lonely
do not last
forever...

birds
know this,
and
that is
why
they
sing.

Don't give up,
don't give in
to feelings
of failure;
doubts
come and
go, just
as
seasons
do ...

when all
that is good
seems lost,
remember that
life is a
circle,
and promise
is on
the
horizon.

If you can
feel the warmth
of the sun
on your face,
or smell the fragrance
of the earth,
or hear the
sparrow's song,

then you will
know that you
are a part of
nature, with your
own uniqueness
and beauty
and reason
for being.

Life is not
always
bright,
but if the
sun can
shine

after the
darkest
storm,
so can
we.

No matter
how cold the wind,
no matter how
dark the day,
there
is warmth
inside a heart
filled with
love
and
understanding.

Nature gives us
warm sunshine,
fragrant breezes and
bird songs to remind us

that no matter how
rough life may
become,
there will always
be times of
gentleness and
peace and
the opportunity
for
growth.

Some days are
better than others,
and some days
are best forgotten;
but as the fading
light marks the
days end,

think on the good
things in life
things innocent and
true, and fall asleep
dreaming of the
promise tomorrow
brings.

When the
cold wind
blows
a chill
through your
heart,
and the world
seems
unforgiving,

Be patient
and persevere,
for always
times of
gentleness
and love
return.

Search the
wind
for your
highest
dream,
then let
your
heart
fly free...

With
courage
and faith
unwavering,
be
all
that you
can
be.

Each day that
dawns brings
promise and
opportunity and
the chance to
make dreams
come
true.

There is
magic
in the moments
between
day
and
night...

as colors
melt away
into twilight,
bringing hope
for a
bright
tomorrow.

You have
within you the
strength to triumph...
you can turn
a stumbling block
into a
stepping stone
that brings
you one step
closer
to
catching
your
dream

If we
possess
the ability
to
dream,
the potential
to fulfill
dreams
also lies
within
us.

Set a goal
and keep on track,
don't let life's
misfortunes make
you doubt
your
course...

press on,
diligence and hard
work never go
unrewarded, and
dreams
really do
come true.

To age
well,
we must
continue to
dream, for
it is reaching
for dreams
that keeps us
forever young
at heart.